EXPANDING FORWARD

Finding Your Way
Back Home To You

EXPANDING FORWARD

Finding Your Way
Back Home To You

Carole Lewitski

Published by Expanding Forward

First Printing: 2017

ISBN: 978-1-365-90132-4

Expanding Forward Publishing

Cover Design by Blue Zoo Creative
www.bluezoocreative.com

This book is dedicated to every soul that yearns to deepen his or her human experience by going on the journey of rediscovering their true authentic SELF.

BE GENTLE WITH YOURSELF...

Listening to that critical voice in our heads, and taking it seriously, takes us completely out of the flow and prevents us from fully living life. And yet, it's so easy to forget that none of that mental chatter has anything to do with who we truly are.

Do you ever catch yourself internally saying, "I thought I dealt with this already! Why is it taking me so long to finally let go?"

What if, instead of being so hard on ourselves, we took a moment, just a moment, to recognize how far we've come.

Maybe it's time to be gentle with ourselves. After all, doing our best, one moment at a time, is truly all we can do.

Don't hold together what must fall apart. The familiar life crumbles so the new life can begin.
~ Bryant McGill

Sometimes we can get so used to being uncomfortable in a situation (job, relationship) that we don't even consider that it could look any other way. Change can be scary, mostly because change brings up the unfamiliar. Fear of the unknown can have such a powerful grip on us, preventing us from moving forward. When things get so uncomfortable, that's usually an indicator that change is being asked of us.

When we start letting go of what we think we know, and open ourselves up to what could be, what shows up is limitless possibilities.

Are you willing to be open to the unfamiliar? Are you willing to receive what is waiting to come into your life? Who knows, you might be surprised to find these changes are not as scary as you thought.

Sometimes we can set false expectations of perfection for ourselves, or our expectations are just so high that we never end up going through with anything. How often do we not take that first step, just because we're scared it's not going to be good enough, or that it won't play out just right? So, we just don't even start….

What is your heart calling you to do? Sometimes it can be as simple as making a phone call to someone who keeps coming up in your mind, or perhaps having a difficult and honest conversation, or maybe it could be signing up for dance lessons or an art class, or writing the book that's been asking to be written so that it can be shared. The hardest step can be that first step, of course, but what's the alternative? Is staying stagnant and perceptively comfortable with what's familiar really that comfortable in the end?

We're all here to be our own unique expression, and when we're finally ready to say, "Here I am!" and really show up every day, truly listening to our heart, then, and only then, does the magic start showing up in our lives. Perhaps it's time to "Create a story worth reading."

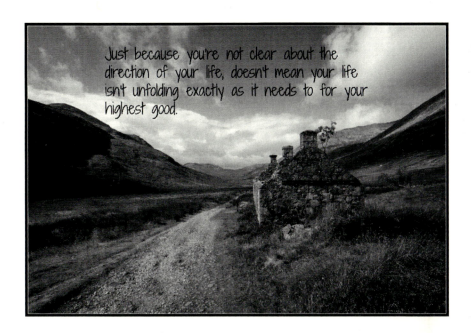

Just because you're not clear about the direction of your life, doesn't mean your life isn't unfolding exactly as it needs to for your highest good.

It can be so easy to get frustrated with life; where we are and where we think we should be (like there's actually a destination). What if there really is no place to get to, other than fully showing up; right here, right now, no matter how messy, icky, or how attached to things we may be. What if we tried not judging that it should look any different than it does?

How often do you hear the expression, "Just let it go," a phrase used so often in spiritual teachings? That phrase has personally frustrated me on a few occasions (OK, maybe several occasions!). In my own head, I have often criticized myself with, "Why can't you just let it go?" From a logical standpoint, it would seem so easy to do just that, especially when you know you're hanging onto something that does not serve your journey. But there is usually so much more at play than what we perceive. Certain aspects of our experience have to play out before we're able to "let it go," and the trick is not to judge how long it takes. Life uses strange means to prepare us for that moment when we can finally wake up and

realize, "We really DO have to let it go," and there is nothing to do but let it all play out. Resistance and judgment of the journey itself are what delay the ultimate surrendering.

When we can come from a place of not judging our life situation, and simply being present to it, even being grateful for it, then that's the sweet spot. And that sweet spot sometimes stinks, or is painful or just plain old complicated. But, it's perfect nonetheless, because guess what, you are so perfect where you are.

And by the way, thank you for showing up and being you, the perfectly imperfect you; because I know that the most heroic of moments occur in the silence of our own hearts. Those moments occur without a witness, and without anyone there to give us a pat on the back and say, "Job well done." So I'm saying it to you now, because we all need to hear it: "Job well done, and thank you for being perfect, exactly where you are."

Slow down and take time to breathe...

Let's face it, life can get pretty crazy sometimes, and it's so easy to get caught up in overwhelm. Whether this overwhelm comes from outside circumstances or from the incessant chatter in our minds (or both, for that matter), we all experience it at some point. In fact, it can become such a "norm" that you might not even consider it could look any other way.

Taking just a few moments during the day to step away from the craziness can really make all the difference, in either your work or personal relationships. And, stepping away does not have to be as complicated as making time for a one-hour yoga class in the morning, an hour of meditation at lunch, and a good, hard workout after work. Taking a step away can be as simple as taking a few deep breaths, pausing before answering a question or email or text, or walking away from a situation, while taking a moment to reflect on how you want to address whatever is presenting. That brief moment can make all the difference. It's going from the default of an immediate response, to allowing yourself to breathe, really breathe, and asking yourself, "How do I want to be, right here, right now?" Each moment defines the next, and if we rush into life, it quickly turns into a blurry mess.

Today is a good day to start putting this into practice; honoring yourself enough to step back, take a moment, and breathe. Watch and see how much flow can return to your life, and the inner peace you will start feeling even if you are surrounded by chaos. It really is that simple. Now go enjoy your crazy life!

Do you have the courage to live the life you know you were meant to live?

A while back, I had the privilege of taking in the Hay House, "I Can Do It," event. They had an amazing panel of inspirational speakers, one of whom was Dr. Wayne Dyer. He started his talk on Saturday morning saying that one of the most common things dying people utter in their last days is, "*I wish I had the courage to live the life I knew I was meant to live.*" During that weekend, I had the chance to hear incredible stories from various other speakers, but that one sentence really stayed with me and continues to be part of my daily reflection.

To live the life I knew I was meant to live: what does that even mean? Maybe it suggests that deep down, if we really stop to take a look, we truly do know why we are here. But we can get so caught up with the extravagant idea that it has to be some epic life mission or world changing vision or action, and that alone prevents us from taking a first step. What if that epic life mission is simply showing up; showing up fully every day as you, not as who you think others want or expect you to be, but simply as you. Grabbing every opportunity to bring more love, more kindness, more compassion, more joy to our own lives, even to our own thoughts, and then that naturally starts showing up in the way we treat others. Wouldn't it stand to reason that, little by little, the world would change through us, and then through others whom we impact?

Sometimes what it takes is a dramatic life event, like being diagnosed with a serious illness, or surviving a vehicle accident, before we finally get motivated to make the changes that we know are needed to live life the way we know we are meant to live it. But what if we don't have to wait until that moment? Because, if we really stop to think about it, every day could very well be our last... so, why don't we start asking ourselves the question right now? *What life am I meant to live?* And start living that life today.

Honest conversations... that's what authentic relationships are made of...

Recently, I have had quite a few difficult and honest conversations, probably because I have finally taken up the courage to speak the truth that my heart contains. I can see why I would often resort to staying silent, though. When we speak the truth about how we feel, there is a chance that it can cause major discomfort in the other person. We can be scared that they will love us less, that they will resent what we say, that they might not understand, that they could judge us, or worse, that we could lose them.

What I had never considered is that perhaps discomfort was exactly what the other person was asking for, on a deep-soul level? It may be that through the discomfort, clarity would finally be able to show up. When I started being okay with others being uncomfortable, and being uncomfortable myself, the more peace I felt inside and the more real I could start being with those around me.

And, in the end, isn't that a deeper expression of love for that person? To honor myself enough, and to honor them enough, to come from a place of being real, no matter what that may look like. To be so willing to be vulnerable and to sit in the discomfort, isn't that the best way to show real love for another, even if what you say might hurt them, upset them, or cause distance between the two of you for a period of time?
On the other hand, staying silent and choosing not to say what is asking to be said, may keep everyone around us seemingly comfortable. But, comfortable doesn't necessarily mean happy or fulfilled or deepening relationships.

What truths do you keep hidden away within your heart? What conversations are waiting to be had? Today is as good a day as any to start honoring yourself and in the end it honors everyone else around you.

The pathway
to awakening to the
truth of who we are
can have some
wicked twists and
turns...

In the last while, I heard from several sources (friends, clients, family members), that they are feeling pushed to their limits. Feeling things that they don't understand, either intense emotion or feeling drawn in and out of a state similar to depression, even when in many cases depression is not a common thing for them.

Some are feeling a deep loneliness; others a longing or void within, and then others are feeling intense anger or sadness. It's difficult when our mind does not have all the answers and, in that space, it's easier to resist it or resent it, and that is when suffering occurs.

What if we were to consider that all of it is happening for our higher good, even if we don't understand it? Is it possible that we are being asked to step up our game, to truly look deeper and start seeing what perhaps we have been avoiding, hiding or suppressing? And wouldn't it stand to reason that when things start coming to the surface, a certain degree of discomfort would show up? Can we be OK with discomfort? Are we willing to go through what we need to go through, even if we don't always understand? What if this loneliness, sadness, anger and/or all of it, is simply our desire to reconnect with the deepest parts of ourselves that have been missing in action for so many years? And what if we are being asked to let go of the aspects of ourselves that simply do not serve anymore?

In the space of not understanding, we get to practice letting go. We get to remember that we are always being taken care of, that we will never be given more than we can handle, and that life is really happening FOR us and not TO us. We also get to reach out to each other and be reminded that we truly are not alone.

Love in its purest form, leaves no room for worry...

It's interesting how worrying about others has so often been a way of saying we care about someone, or even a way of showing them that we love them. But if we believe we are being taken care of at all times, that everything happens for a reason, and that we are all being presented only with what we can handle, where exactly does worry fit in?

Is it possible that when we worry about others (their life choices, spiritual well-being, their health or financial situation), perhaps it's simply a very convenient way of distracting ourselves from living our own lives? When our mind is elsewhere, preoccupied by other people's lives, choices and situations, how can we have the time to look in the mirror and see clarity for ourselves?

Because, if we take the time to do that, maybe we would get to ask ourselves the questions that really matter: "How am I showing up in my own life, with the most love that I have to offer? How can I be a better person? Do I acknowledge that I am being taken care of always, and that I have my own inner wisdom to guide me every step of the way?" When we do that, it also empowers others and reminds them that they are not alone; they will get through whatever life hands them and that all is well, even if, at times, it might not look the way we would want it to.

This translates into a much deeper love towards others than if we spent our time worrying about them.

What if there were a deeper form of love available that leaves no room for worry? How freeing would that be for everyone involved?

You are enough... Embrace YOUR magnificence!

Have you ever noticed how easy it can be to get caught up in the trap of seeking validation for our worth based on how others see us? For many years, I found myself measuring my own value based on how much people around me appreciated me or approved of me. I figured that if they saw me as valuable, then I must be valuable. But to keep up with that, I had to always make sure I was in everyone's good books; that I was the friend everyone wished to have, the daughter who made my parents proud, the wife who seemed too good to be true, or the mother who outdid herself in every way. What a reputation to maintain, and how exhausting to be assuming and assessing what everyone around me expected of me, or wanted/wished me to be.

It struck me one day when someone took the time to ask me the powerful question, "Have you ever considered that you are enough just as you are?" This slowly started brewing inside of me, reflections that maybe, just maybe, I was actually good enough exactly the way I was. That even if I had to say "no" to someone, or not be there for everyone who turned to me for help, or to be all the things I had worked so hard to be; even if I couldn't measure up to all of that, it changed nothing about who I am. I was still whole and complete and still worthy of love.

Just the simple fact that we exist; that in itself makes us good enough. We can finally stop being who we think everyone around us wants us to be, and start just being the best version of who we are. After all, we are divine expressions of creation; how could that possibly not be good enough?

Embrace your own magnificence and by doing so, you might be surprised to see that everyone around you was waiting for that version of you all along.

Only THIS moment matters...

So how about let's make it worth remembering...

The best advice I ever received was when I was a young mother, visiting my husband's grandmother. She is a World War II survivor and spent part of her life in a displaced person camp. All of the wisdom she was able to pass on to me during those years, when I was transitioning to life as a woman and mother, is something I cherish to this day.

There is one particular piece of advice that stands out the most. She said to me, "When you wake up in the morning, look at what is right in front of you. Don't think about how difficult your night was, or worry about what might happen during the day. Just look at the moment right in front of you and be grateful." I never took lightly what she said, given what she had been through and overcome.

Those words helped me tremendously over the years, and still give me strength on difficult days. Is there really anything else that exists but what is right here in front of us? Why preoccupy ourselves with what we wish it had looked like, or even what we hope it will look like? All that does is create frustration, disappointment and, oftentimes, a feeling of being overwhelmed. When we can look to the moment right in front of us, we come to realize that nothing else, truly nothing else, matters and nothing else exists. Then we get to ask ourselves the questions, "Is there anything for me to do? Is there anything for me to say? And how much love can I emanate in this very moment?" As tough as some moments can be, just remember we are never given more than we can handle, and we are being taken care of always.

Go be curious with your life, find what makes your heart excited and do more of that.

There was a time when I used to compare myself to others and their incredible talents and thought, "They are so lucky, because I just wasn't born with creativity." I was so busy admiring what everyone else was up to that I was completely oblivious to my own creative genius.

We all have access to that creativity. It's only when we start comparing ourselves to others that we miss the gifts that we've been given. "Oh, not me! I don't have a creative bone in my body." How many of us have said that before? But here's the thing; creativity comes in so many shapes and forms… gardening, baking, writing, singing, cooking, dancing, drawing, playing instruments, photography, painting, designing of every kind, and it goes on and on….

Why should you care to dive into your creative genius? Well, maybe because that is where your heart is, and that also is where the purest expression of your essence comes through. In that space is where we become alive. Creativity and love are so closely tied that the more creativity we allow to flow through us, the more love can show up.

Just a few days ago, I heard a good friend of mine utter these very wise words, "Creativity is our quickest connection to the Divine." I agree fully!

So be curious with your life; find what makes your heart excited, and do more of that.

Surrender to the flow of your life, whatever the flow of that moment may be.

It is so easy to get frustrated, and even discouraged, some days; wanting to throw in the towel, the "awakening towel." LOL. I've heard so many comments of late about how done they are, and just want to go back to the way it was before. The real question to ask is, could we actually ever go back?

Being accountable for your own journey is huge, and it's freeing all at the same time. Being in the driver's seat for your own experience is empowering and requires going through challenging periods. What's good to remember is that through each challenge lies an opportunity for growth.

"Along the way, we meet the right souls to support us and love us through these difficult periods. I've thought at times, when I've felt crushed by the weight of life's challenges, in a state of wanting to curl up and give up on it all; that maybe, to be challenged to this degree is actually a compliment, because, as the saying goes, 'You only get given what you can handle.' Or maybe it is also because the Universe not only has confidence in us, but is right there supporting us every step of the way. When we surface from the darkness, your soul is strengthened by the purifying fire of adversity." (excerpt from the book I am in the process of writing, *A Kiss From Eternity*)

Just remember that, even in the most difficult and painful situations, beauty is at its core, and that beauty is the unfolding of who you truly are.

Learn to embrace the mysteries of LOVE...

It's one thing to love those around us who are easy to love, receptive to it, and with whom our relationship has ease and flow. But what about those individuals in our lives who aren't as easy to love? Where do they fit in, and how is it possible to still feel the gifts that love has to offer?

When we are triggered by people, be it our children, our co-workers or even (hold tight for this one), our partner, what do we do with that? Do we get defensive, do we take it personally, do we close up, or do we promise ourselves that we won't be "that vulnerable" ever again? Those silent promises are very real, and they impact us in a big way. When we close our hearts and protect ourselves, we close ourselves off to, yes, perhaps the potential pain and hurt, but we also close ourselves off to the expansion that love brings into our experience, and the deep soul learning involved. That part of love is not as tangible, and it certainly does not offer instant gratification.

And we might say to ourselves, "Love should feel good, should make me smile, should boost my spirit, should make me feel alive and passionate, should, should, should...." When we are ready to drop all the expectations of what love "should" look like, it then leaves room for love to show up in whatever way it is meant to show up for us. And sometimes it's not pretty and sometimes it hurts. But other times, when we can overcome and look beyond the behaviors and ask ourselves, "What am I being shown about me in all of this; how can I grow and what changes can I make?" Then, and only then, can we start to really see the hidden treasures that love has to offer, beyond what we've been led to believe in romantic movies or love stories.

Love comes in all shapes and sizes; it is mysterious, unexpected, and uniquely designed for each of our own individual journeys. Try diving into all the loves in your life as though you have absolutely nothing to lose. Because that's the truth; there is nothing to lose and so much to gain. Only when we realize this, will we be given the gifts that words cannot describe, the mind cannot understand, and only the language of the heart can feel.

Every day is a good day to love!

CHANGE IS SIMPLY A DOORWAY TOWARDS NEW ADVENTURES...

Sometimes life surprises us by having dramatic changes show up. It can really shake us up, and fear can quickly make its way into the picture. When things feel stable and predictable, we can easily get pulled into thinking that we are in control of our life, when in fact that is simply an illusion.

Imagine the freedom of living life knowing that a higher wisdom is overseeing our life, and that we are safe at all times. That even when unexpected things, like losing a job or becoming bedridden with sickness, happen, it would be happening FOR us and not TO us. What if all those surprises life throws at us are there to encourage us to stop and to be open to something else that we are meant to experience? Is it possible to consider that perhaps life is simply showing us a "redirect," and that this change can be a gift rather than something to fear?

We really, truly, are being taken care of at every moment. If we are right here, right now in this moment, it is precisely because we've overcome the impossible many times over during our life.

And most of us have survived through surprising circumstances.

When change shows up and takes us by surprise, we can either resist it, fear it and lose sleep over it, or we can say, "Thank you", knowing that not only will we overcome, but there's a good chance that exciting new adventures are waiting for us right around the corner. All we have to do is let life show us all it has in store for us, one adventure at a time.

What risks are you willing to take?

When I talk about risks, I'm not talking about jumping out of airplanes, although that is fun as heck. I'm talking about risks of the heart. Taking the leap, jumping in to see it all and, scarier than that, letting others see it, too. Yup, that is one scary ride…. But, something to consider is that staying stuck where it seemingly feels "safe" is not a better option.

So, where in your life can you dive in deeper? With whom can you start showing up as the truer version of yourself? Who in your life have you been morphing yourself for, out of fear that they might judge you? We never do anyone a favor by showing up as an altered version of ourselves. If they chose to have you in their lives, it's precisely because they want to see all of you.

So, here's the thing; you can sit at the doorway or you can take the leap. It's totally up to you! But, man, is it ever amazing when we get a glimpse of the other side… it truly is where freedom begins.

Thriving involves expanding into life while looking for blessings and how to contribute, instead of simply trying to avoid suffering by changing your circumstances.

~ Jennifer Hough

When going through tough times, it's easy and it's normal to want to run away from the pain or the suffering. What if there were a different way? What if we asked ourselves these questions:

Have I been feeling gratitude for all the things that I do have?

How can I dig deeper and emanate more love, even when I don't feel like it?

How can I be more present to this very moment?

Could I approach others in my life with more love and compassion?

When we give others what we ourselves feel we are lacking, it comes back to us exponentially. Like the example of the homeless person offering what little he has to someone in greater need.

Where in our lives can we give more? How in our everyday moments can we contribute in a deeper way? Sometimes it's as simple as being so very present to someone talking to us, needing a non-judgmental listening ear. And in those moments, when the magic unfolds, maybe, just maybe, our sufferings won't feel so heavy.

To live in hearts we leave behind
is not to die.
~ Thomas Campbell

I was writing a chapter in my book the other morning and the topic happened to be on death and dying. I decided to take a break and go for a walk to clear my head, and ended up running into a friend who lives a few streets down from me. As we were catching up on our lives, she started telling me that her father passed away a few weeks ago. And, because I don't believe in coincidences and I had just been writing on that very topic that morning, my heart cracked wide open as I listened to her tell me of this incredible experience she had in his last moments. She stood at his side as he took his last breath, and the look in her eyes as she told me about it, brought me right there in that moment, and I could feel the mystery and magic of it all.

I haven't lost a parent yet. I don't know what that feels like, but I can say that as I listened to her share with me such intimate details, my heart was humbled with gratitude for the wisdom she had to offer. She went on to say that although she clearly felt him gone from his body, she didn't for one moment feel him gone from her, and that he simply continued to be. As she stood by his beautiful body, it also became so clear to her how our body is a vessel, a powerful vessel, that houses our essence or our soul, but it is not who we are. And that the things that we might preoccupy ourselves with, worries of every kind, are so unimportant because, when all is said and done, and we reach the end of this journey, who we are still remains. And we get to ask ourselves the question, what really mattered all along?

It was so powerful being a witness to her experience, which has marked her life, and now mine as well. When all the details and the things that preoccupy us are removed, all that remains that is worth our time and energy is love and relationships. If we knew that our time of transition was soon coming, who would we love more, and what might we say that hasn't been said?

People are doing the best that they can from their own level of consciousness.
~ Deepak Chopra

Do you ever come across someone who just rubs you the wrong way? Who triggers you or talks to you in a way that leaves you wondering, "What the heck did I do? What is his/her problem?" Before you know it, you get pulled into the drama, and soon their issues become your issues. We can so easily make it about ourselves, when maybe all along it has little or even nothing to do with us. What if there were a different way of experiencing situations like those?

What if there were only two simple questions to ask…

1) Is this even about me?
2) What is there for me to see in all of this?

It's a clever distraction when we busy ourselves thinking how wrong the other person was, and judge their way of being. It distracts us from looking at ourselves. It's good to remember that everyone is doing his or her best with what they have, and what they know at the time. Sometimes that shows up as someone's being a jerk and sometimes, let's be real, we're the one being the jerk. So, maybe if we can stop for a moment, recognize that other people's behaviors are really not about us, and then ask ourselves what there is for us to see. Then maybe, in that moment, instead of it being a confrontation or a reason to get pulled into drama, it can become an opportunity for us to see how we can show up with more love in our own lives. We're all in this together, after all.

How much time do you spend trying to impress others, or trying to keep a good reputation with those around you? What has that cost you in your life? What things have you compromised, or what choices have you avoided making, for fear of getting judged or misunderstood?

Sometimes our journeys can take us down twists and turns that are not what we would expect or even wish for ourselves, but it really is what shows up. What also can show up is the fear that others might not understand, or might judge us for the actions we feel called to take, or tough decisions we might need to make. Our own journey can be difficult for even ourselves to understand at times, so how can we expect others to support and understand us?

What in your own life do you know with all your heart that you feel called to do, but feel scared of being misunderstood or judged? When will listening to your heart, or your soul's voice, become more important than what anyone else might think? After all, it has the wisdom to see things from a much higher perspective, and will never steer you wrong.

Isn't it time to start honoring your own soul's journey?

Set yourself free

from the cage of
victimhood...

I remember at one point in my life, standing outside my home, looking up at the sky in desperation and asking, "Why? Why are you doing this to me? I don't know how much more I can take!" I was filled with disbelief as to what was showing up in my life, and confused as to why someone up there had what seemed like a twisted sense of humor. In that moment, feeling very much like a victim, while also wanting to make sure I was blaming the right party, I stopped and wondered, who else, other than God or the Universe, would know all the secrets of my heart? Who else could so cleverly design events to show up that would push me to my limit? And, to my surprise, the answer that showed up was "Me!"

Now, why would I ask for these challenges and obstacles to show up? Why would I put myself through such difficult situations? The only sensible explanation that came up is that maybe, on a soul level, we are all asking to be challenged in ways that can best contribute to our spiritual and personal growth. That perhaps all of it, the whole package, the joyful and blissful moments, as well as the extremely uncomfortable ones, are there to enhance and push us to our maximum potential.

Being a victim allows us to stay stuck. and not to be accountable for anything in our own lives. When we blame others, or blame our life circumstances, it only acts as a convenient way of avoiding looking at ourselves and making the necessary changes to improve our lives. Seeing it all as perfect and exactly as it should be, on the other hand, becomes absolutely empowering.

What are you feeling victim of in your own life? Is it your mother who couldn't be who you wanted her to be? Your spouse, who doesn't meet your needs? Your children, who stress you out beyond belief? Or your boss, who demands too much of you?

What would it look like to live your life without being a victim of anyone or anything, anymore? Are you ready to start experiencing the freedom that exists when you're in control of your own life and your own destiny?

What does trust have to do with Love?

www.expandingforward.com

Who can we really trust? How many of us have been burned, hurt, disappointed or betrayed? How many times are we willing to put ourselves through that before we make the final decision, "I will never trust anyone again…," or worse yet, "I will never love someone that much again.…"

What is trust anyway? And at what point does a person become worthy of our trust? Is it when they've had a "clean" record for X amount of months or years? When you really stop to think about it, trust, in and of itself, insinuates the potentiality of betrayal or deceit. There is this expectancy of pain that is looming around every corner. Perhaps another question to ask is; can we even trust ourselves? And trust ourselves to what, exactly? To be perfect? To never screw up? To never twist or alter the truth?

Maybe the only thing we can trust is that yes, we will make mistakes; yes, we will deceive, we will disappoint and, guess what, others will do all of those things as well. But more importantly, the question to ask is, "Will that stop me from loving others, or can I love anyway?"

It may feel safe to close off your heart so that you won't be wounded again, but why stay in such a lonely space, when so many out there are waiting to love and be loved by you? If we wait for that "perfect" person whom we can trust one hundred percent before we love and let love in, the only person we short change is ourselves. Staying "safe" is so overrated. So how about we just choose to love anyway.

What matters most is showing up as the best version of ourselves in all moments.

www.wexpandingforward.com

I took part in a beautiful celebration at our children's school the other day, and was touched by what I experienced. To be able to spend two hours surrounded by innocence and beauty was so refreshing. Being around the simplicity of children is always a great reminder of what really matters.

No matter what might be going on in the world, worrying and panicking only perpetrates more fear, and we certainly don't need to contribute more fear to the collective energy. When fear, apprehension and anxiety show up in our lives, the question to ask is, "What is there for me to do?" The answer to that is often, if not always, right in front of us. From there, we can ask ourselves what is actually in our control to change or affect; perhaps it's the way that we are with our children, our co-workers, our aging parents, our partner, or anyone who crosses our path throughout the day, for that matter. How are we showing up for those people in our lives? Are we choosing kindness over "being right?" Are we discerning when to speak and when it's best to be silent and simply listen? Are we taking a moment to do some introspection, checking in to make sure we are showing up as the best version of ourselves in all moments, even if that looks different from moment to moment?

Life will keep bringing us circumstances that can seem too much to handle, but it serves to test our willingness to believe that we are being taken care of at all times, and that there is a higher power overseeing all of it (the world's problems, as well as our own personal struggles). No matter how challenging, chaotic, or gloom-and-doom things may seem, we are being taken care of, always.

And if life still feels too overwhelming, then that's when it's important to reach out to someone who can help. No one needs to go through any difficulties alone. Let's not forget; we're all in this together, after all.

Treat yourself with the love and compassion you would a child in distress...

Have you ever taken the time to listen to the voice in your head? When you act in a way that doesn't measure up to your expectations of yourself, what kind of conversations show up inside of you? If you spoke those same words to a five-year-old child in distress, would it be considered kind? Or would it be considered abusive?

Do you think it ever works to bully ourselves into becoming a better person? Or to berate and judge the heck out of ourselves until we change?

When you are going through big changes or going through difficult times, or when you realize you've behaved in a way that you regret, the last thing you need to hear is a critical voice, or a voice that tells you that you should know better, or that you failed again. In fact, what you need most is for someone to be loving and compassionate and hold you in their arms, reminding you that you are loved and that you will get through this.

What if you could be that person for yourself? What if you could hold the small child inside of you in your arms and remind the innocence within you that all is well, and that you are doing your best in every moment?

When we start choosing only words of love and compassion toward ourselves, this contributes to making our world a better place, and this begins by silencing the one bully we have control over.

Show up for yourself in the most loving way, and that will shine through you and how you show up for others in your life.

About the Author

Carole Lewitski is a Licensed Awakening Coach, speaker and writer who specializes in assisting individuals overcome fear or any limiting beliefs keeping them stuck or unable to move forward within all areas of their lives. Carole has a deep desire to empower people to reconnect with the truth of who they are.

She is a heart centered, intuitive mother of 8 beautiful beings of light, and has learned to embody pure compassion for the human journey through her experiences as a mother and from working with clients of all ages and all walks of life. She stays actively connected to her innate healing abilities through her gifts as an energy worker and Certified Awakening Coach. Carole's biggest passion in life is relationship with Divinity and connection to what's possible. She loves people and thrives in having honest conversations with whomever crosses her path. Her mission and passion is to be all that she came here to be; to live, dance and lean in to all that life presents to her and in the process, creating a space for those around her to feel safe to do the same.

Website: www.expandingforward.com
Follow Carole on Twitter: @CaroleLewitski
Facebook: Carole Forest Lewitski

To join the Expanding Forward community online go to the EXPANDING FORWARD Facebook page.

To get in touch with Carole for a Free Discovery Session visit her at:

www.expandingforward.com/book-online